Published by Mz. Kim Productions
4263 Tierra Rejada Rd #151
Moorpark, CA 93021
www.mzkimproductions.com
ISBN: 978-1-962106-04-7

Printed in United States of America
First Printing: August 2023
Date of Copyright: July 5, 2023

Cover design by Veronika Wilson (TechflamesLLC)
Illustrations by Veronika Wilson (TechflamesLLC)

For permissions, please contact: Mz. Kim Productions
4263 Tierra Rejada Rd #151
Moorpark, CA 93021
www.mzkimproductions.com
mzkimproductions@gmail.com

I0457565

Once upon a time, there was a little boy named Gio. He loved playing with his toys and exploring the world aroun him.

Momma, swing me higher!

Hold on tight, Gio! You are my little superstar.

Momma, why are you my guardian angel?

Because, my precious Gio, I will always watch over you, even when I'm not physically here.

Momma, what happens when someone becomes a guardian angel?

When someone becomes a guardian angel, they join Jesus in heaven and continue to spread love and watch over their loved ones on Earth.

Momma, why did you have to go to heaven?

Sometimes, our bodies become tired, but our love remains forever. I am always with you, Gio, in your heart and as your guardian angel.

Momma, how can I feel your love?

See those twinkling stars, Gio? Each one carries a message of love from me to you. Whenever you miss me, look up at the stars, and you'll feel my love surrounding you.

Momma, can my friends have guardian angels too?

Absolutely, Gio! Each one of your friends has their very own guardian angel, just like you. They are always there, guiding and protecting them.

Momma, can I still talk to you?

Even though you can't see me, I'm always listening, Gio. Share your thoughts, dreams, and worries with me through your prayers. I will be there,holding your hand.

Momma, can I plant a flower for you?

That's a beautiful idea, Gio! Every time you see that flower, remember it's a symbol of our love. It will remind you that I'm always near, cheering you on.

Goodnight, Momma. I love you!

As Gio closed his eyes, he felt a gentle presence watching over him. His guardian angel, his momma Ebony, was always there, keeping him safe and warm.

Good morning, Momma! I know you're here with me.

Good morning, my sweet Gio. I'm here to guide you through each day, to wrap you in love, and to remind you that you are never alone.

Thank you, Momma, for teaching me about love and the love of Jesus. I will share that love with everyone I meet.

Goodbye, Momma! I'll always feel your love and carry it in my heart.

And so, Gio grew up knowing that his momma, his guardian angel, would always be by his side. He shared her love and the love of Jesus with others, spreading joy and kindness wherever he went. And in his heart, he knew that love would never fade.

AUTHOR PAGE

I am a passionate and dedicated writer who believes in the power of storytelling to inspire, educate, and bring people together. With a deep appreciation for the written word, [Author's Name] strives to create stories that touch the hearts and minds of readers of all ages.

Having a background in theology and counseling, I brings a unique perspective to writing, often exploring themes of resilience, growth, and the human spirit. With a focus on empathy and understanding, I aim to create narratives that resonate with readers, offering comfort and guidance through life's challenges.

I am particularly drawn to stories that celebrate diversity, inclusivity, and the power of community. Through their writing, they seek to promote empathy and compassion, reminding readers of the importance of understanding and embracing our differences.

With a love for children's literature, I am dedicated to crafting stories that captivate young minds and ignite their imaginations. Believing that literature plays a vital role in shaping the lives of children, I strives to create books that entertain, educate, and inspire young readers to dream big and embrace their uniqueness.

Thank you for visiting the author's page of. Stay tuned for updates on current and upcoming projects, as well as insights into the creative process. Connect with [Author's Name] on social media to join in the journey of storytelling and to be a part of a community that celebrates the power of words.

DEDICATION

This book is dedicated to all the brave children and families who have experienced loss.

To those who have faced the pain of saying goodbye to a loved one, this book is for you. Your strength and resilience in the face of unimaginable sorrow is truly inspiring.

May this story provide comfort and solace during your healing journey. May it remind you that love transcends boundaries and that the memories of those we have lost will forever live on in our hearts.

To the children who have had to navigate the confusing emotions that come with grief, know that you are not alone. This book is here to hold your hand and guide you through the difficult process of understanding and accepting loss.

To the families who have supported and embraced each other during times of sorrow, your unity and love are a shining light in the darkest of times. May this book serve as a reminder of the strength that lies within your bonds.

In honoring your resilience, courage, and unwavering love, we dedicate "Gio's Guardian Angel" to you. May it bring you comfort, healing, and hope as you continue to cherish the memories of those who have touched your lives.

With deepest empathy and heartfelt support,

GIO'S GUARDIAN ANGEL 2
OFFERS SEVERAL EDUCATIONAL VALUES FOR YOUNG READERS

1. **Understanding Loss and Grief:** The book sensitively addresses the topic of loss and grief, helping children understand the concept of death and the emotions associated with it. It teaches them that while a loved one may physically be gone, their love and presence can still be felt.

2. **Exploring Spirituality:** The book introduces the idea of guardian angels and their role in protecting and guiding individuals. It opens up conversations about spirituality and the belief in higher powers, allowing children to explore their own thoughts and beliefs.

3. **Expressing Emotions:** "Gio's Guardian Angel" encourages children to express their emotions and talk about their feelings. It shows them that it is okay to feel sad, miss someone, and ask questions about life and death.

4. **Promoting Empathy and Kindness:** Through Gio's journey, the book emphasizes the importance of empathy and kindness towards others. It teaches children to share love, support, and compassion with those around them, just as Gio's guardian angel does for him.

5. **Connecting with Nature:** The book incorporates natural elements like stars, flowers, and sunshine to symbolize love and the presence of a guardian angel. It encourages children to appreciate and connect with nature, fostering a sense of wonder and mindfulness.

6. **Cultivating Faith and Hope:** "Gio's Guardian Angel" instills faith and hope in children by showing them that they are never alone, even in difficult times. It teaches them to believe in something beyond themselves and find comfort in the thought that they are always loved and protected.

Overall, the educational value of "Gio's Guardian Angel" lies in its ability to help children navigate complex emotions, explore spirituality, and cultivate empathy, kindness, and hope.